—DEDICATED TO —

THE LOVING MEMORY OF MY MOTHER,

GENEVIEVE NELSON ARNOLD,

WHO ALWAYS ADDED SPARKLE TO MY LIFE.

— ACKNOWLEDGEMENTS —

PHOTOS BY

JUDIE WHITE

BILL WHITE PAGE 7

SALLY CROWELL PAGE 25

JULIA COFFMAN PAGE 35

SCOTT CROWELL PAGE 37

SIGRID STONE PAGE 55

—A SPECIAL THANKS TO —

ALL YOU FAITHFUL PRAYER WARRIORS, ENCOURAGERS, AND

FINANCIAL SUPPORTERS. WITHOUT YOU THIS BOOK

WOULD BE ONLY A DREAM.

Your word is a
lamp to my feet
and a light for
my path.

■ PSALM 119:105

Celebrate
His Love

Judie White

With God all
things are possible—
Judie White

COPYRIGHT © 2003 JUDIE WHITE

DESIGNED BY JANIE DELANEY

SCRIPTURE TAKEN FROM THE
HOLY BIBLE: NEW INTERNATIONAL VERSION®. NIV®.
COPYRIGHT © 1973, 1978, 1984
BY INTERNATIONAL BIBLE SOCIETY.
USED BY PERMISSION OF ZONDERVAN.

THE NIV AND NEW INTERNATIONAL VERSION TRADEMARKS
ARE REGISTERED IN THE UNITED STATES PATENT AND TRADEMARK OFFICE
BY INTERNATIONAL BIBLE SOCIETY.

PUBLISHED IN THE UNITED STATES OF AMERICA BY:
SCRIPTURE IMAGES
6656 CHADWICK DRIVE, SAVAGE, MINNESOTA 55378
612-916-6987

ISBN 0-9729367-0-X

"Be still, and know
that I am God."

■ PSALM 46:10

Trust in the Lord
with all your heart and
lean not on your
own understanding;
in all your ways
acknowledge him,
and he will make your
paths straight.

■ PROVERBS 3:5-6

The Lord is compassionate and gracious, slow to anger, abounding in love. For as high as the heavens are above the earth, so great is his love for those who fear him; as far as the east is from the west, so far has he removed our transgressions from us.

■ PSALM 103:8,11,12

From the rising of
the sun to the place
where is sets,
the name of the Lord
is to be praised.

■ PSALM 113:3

This is the day
the Lord has made;
let us rejoice and
be glad in it.

■ PSALM 118:24

I meditate on all your
works and consider what your
hands have done.
I spread out my hands
to you; my soul thirsts for you
like a parched land.

■ Psalm 143:5-6

I lift up my eyes to the
hills...where does
my help come from?

My help comes from
the Lord, the Maker of
heaven and earth.

■ PSALM 121:1-2

Give thanks to
the Lord,
for he is good;
his love
endures forever.

■ PSALM 106:1

thanks

All the days

ordained for me were

written in your book

before one of them

came to be.

■ PSALM 139:16

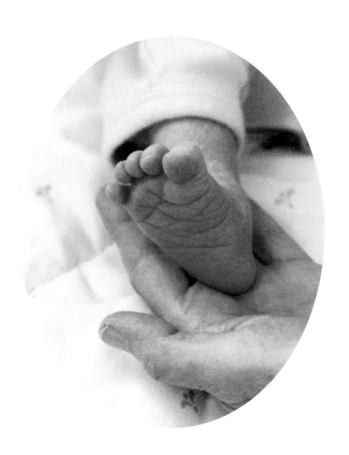

For you created my
inmost being;
you knit me together in
my mother's womb.
I praise you because I
am fearfully and
wonderfully
made…

■ PSALM 139:13,14

"For I know the plans
I have for you,"
declares the Lord,
"plans to prosper you
and not to harm you,
plans to give you hope
and a future."

■ JEREMIAH 29:11

hope

If the Lord delights in
a man's way, he makes
his steps firm;
though he stumble,
he will not fall,
for the Lord upholds
him with his hand.

■ PSALM 37:23-24

Let the morning
bring me word of your
unfailing love,
for I have put my
trust in you.

■ PSALM 143:8

The Lord your God himself will
cross over ahead of you.
Be strong and courageous.
Do not be afraid or terrified...
for the Lord your God goes
with you; he will never leave
you nor forsake you.

■ DEUTERONOMY 31:3,6

The Lord is my strength
and my shield;
my heart trusts in him,
and I am helped.

My heart leaps for joy
and I will give thanks
to him in song.

■ PSALM 28:7

joy

When I said,
"My foot is slipping,"
your love, O Lord,
supported me.

When anxiety was
great within me, your
consolation brought
joy to my soul.

■ PSALM 94:18,19

Great is the Lord and most
worthy of praise; his greatness
no one can fathom.

One generation will commend your
works to another; they will tell of
your mighty acts. They will celebrate
your abundant goodness and
joyfully sing of your
righteousness.

■ PSALM 145:3,4,7

celebrate

After fasting forty days and forty nights, he was hungry.

The tempter came to him and said, "If you are the Son of God, tell these stones to become bread."

Jesus answered, "It is written: 'Man does not live on bread alone, but on every word that comes from the mouth of God.'"

■ MATTHEW 4:2-4

Jesus said to Simon,
"Don't be afraid; from
now on you will
catch men."

So they pulled their
boats up on shore,
left everything and
followed him.

■ LUKE 5:10-11

"Blessed are the pure in heart, for they will see God."

■ MATTHEW 5:8—

"Let your

light shine before men,

that they may see

your good deeds and

praise your Father

in heaven."

■ MATTHEW 5:16

shine

"When you pray,
go into your room,
close the door and pray
to your Father,
who is unseen.

Then your Father,
who sees what is
done in secret,
will reward you."

■ MATTHEW 6:6

"Do not store up for yourselves treasures on earth, where moth and rust destroy, and where thieves break in and steal.

But store up for yourselves treasures in heaven, where moth and rust do not destroy, and where thieves do not break in and steal.

For where your treasure is, there your heart will be also.

■ Matthew 6:19-21

"And why do you worry
about clothes?
See how the lilies of
the field grow.
They do not labor or spin.

Yet I tell you that not even
Solomon in all his splendor was
dressed like one of these."

■ MATTHEW 6:28-29

"Ask and it will be given to you;

seek and you will find;

knock and the door will be

opened to you..."

◼ MATTHEW 7:7

"Come to me, all you who are weary and burdened, and I will give you rest."

■ MATTHEW 11:28

He replied, "I tell you the truth,
if you have faith as small as
a mustard seed, you can say to
this mountain, 'Move from here
to there' and it will move.
Nothing will be impossible for you."

■ MATTHEW 17:20

faith

"My sheep listen to my voice;
I know them, and they follow me.
I give them eternal life, and
they shall never perish;
no one can snatch them
out of my hand."

■ JOHN 10:27-28

"But God chose the fooolish things
of the world to shame the wise;
God chose the weak things
of the world to shame the strong.
He chose the lowly things of this
world and the despised things
...and the things that are not
...to nullify the things that are,
so that no one may
boast before him.
Let him who boasts boast
in the Lord."

■ 1 CORINTHIANS 1:27-29-31

Remember this:
Whoever sows sparingly
will also reap sparingly,
and whoever sows generously
will also reap generously.

■ 2 CORINTHIANS 9:6

I am convinced that neither death nor life, neither angels nor demons, neither the present nor the future, nor any powers, neither height nor depth, nor anything else in all creation, will be able to separate us from the love of God that is in Christ Jesus our Lord.

■ ROMANS 8:38-39

May the God of hope
fill you with all joy and peace
as you trust in him, so that
you may overflow with hope
by the power of the
Holy Spirit.

■ ROMANS 15:13

overflow

The fruit of the Spirit is
love.....joy.....peace
patience.....kindness
goodness.....faithfulness
gentleness and
self-control.....

■ GALATIONS 5:22-23

"In your anger do not sin":

Do not let the sun

go down while you

are still angry.....

■ Ephesians 4:26

Nothing in all creation is hidden
from God's sight.

Everything is uncovered
and laid bare before the eyes
of him to whom we must
give account.

■ Hebrews 4:13

Now faith is being sure of
what we hope for
and certain of
what we do not see.

■ HEBREWS 11:1

"The grass withers and the flowers fall, but The word of the Lord stands forever."

■ 1 PETER 1:24,25

Dear friends,
let us love one another,
for love comes
from God.

■ 1 JOHN 4:7

love

Love is patient, love is kind.
It does not envy, it does not boast,
it is not proud. It is not rude,
it is not self-seeking, it is not easily
angered, it keeps no record of
wrongs. Love does not delight
in the evil but rejoices with the truth.
It always protects, always trusts,
always hopes, always perseveres.

■ I Corinthians 13:4-7

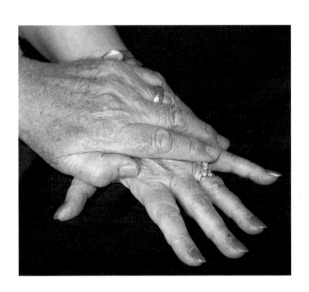

This is how we know what love is:
Jesus Christ laid down
his life for us.

■ 1 John 3:16

If you confess with your mouth,
"Jesus is Lord," and believe
in your heart that God
raised him from the dead,
you will be saved.

For it is with your heart that
you believe and are justified, and
it is with your mouth that you
confess and are saved.

Romans 10:9-10

"Come now, let us reason together," says the Lord.

"Though your sins are like scarlet, they shall be white as snow..."

■ Isaiah 1:18

...It is time to seek
the Lord.

■ Hosea 10:12

seek

"Therefore go and make disciples
of all nations, baptizing them
in the name of the Father and
of the Son and of the Holy Spirit,
and teaching them to obey
everything I have commanded you.

And surely I am with you always,
to the very end of the age."

■ Matthew 28:19-20—

Now may the Lord of peace himself give you peace at all times and in every way.

The Lord be with all of you.

■ 2 Thessalonians 3:16

The Lord be with all of you.

Jesus Loves You!

JESUS LOVES YOU JUST AS YOU ARE, WHOEVER YOU ARE, AND WHEREVER YOU ARE.

2 PETER 3:9 SAYS,

"HE IS PATIENT WITH YOU, NOT WANTING ANYONE TO PERISH, BUT EVERYONE COME TO REPENTANCE." JESUS OFFERS HIMSELF AS A FREE GIFT TO ALL WHO RECOGNIZE THEIR NEED OF A SAVIOR. IF YOU DESIRE TO ACCEPT HIS OFFER OF FORGIVENESS AND SALVATION....I INVITE YOU TO GO TO HIM IN PRAYER.

DEAR LORD JESUS,

I KNOW THAT I AM A SINNER WHO NEEDS YOUR FORGIVENESS. I BELIEVE YOU DIED TO PAY THE PENALTY FOR MY SINS. THANK YOU FOR YOUR FREE GIFT OF SALVATION. PLEASE COME INTO MY LIFE AND GUIDE ME AS I LEARN TO LOVE, TRUST AND FOLLOW YOU. IN YOUR PRECIOUS NAME, AMEN.

IF YOU PRAYED THIS PRAYER, YOU CAN NOW LIVE WITH THE ASSURANCE AND CONFIDENCE THAT YOU BELONG TO HIM FOREVER. JOHN 3:16 SAYS, "FOR GOD SO LOVED THE WORLD THAT HE GAVE HIS ONE AND ONLY SON, THAT WHOEVER BELIEVES IN HIM SHALL NOT PERISH BUT HAVE ETERNAL LIFE."

WELCOME TO GOD'S FAMILY!!